Ten Poems
of Francis Ponge
Translated by Robert Bly

— & —

Ten Poems of Robert Bly
Inspired by the Poems
of Francis Ponge

*Ten Poems
of Francis Ponge
Translated by Robert Bly*

———————— ————————

*Ten Poems of Robert Bly
Inspired by the Poems
of Francis Ponge*

Riverview, New Brunswick

ACKNOWLEDGEMENTS: Some of Robert Bly's poems and his translations of Francis Ponge's poems first appeared in *Germination, Caliban, Chelsea, Inroads, Parabola*, and in the anthology called *News of the Universe*. We are grateful to the editors of these respective publications for permission to print the poems and translations here.

The following original poems by Francis Ponge © Editions Gallimard: Excerpts from LE PARTI PRIS DES CHOSES (1942): Les arbres se défont à l'intérieur d'une sphère de brouillard - Les mûres - La fin de l'automne - L'huître - La bougie - Les plaisirs de la porte - Les trois boutiques - Pluie. Excerpts from PIECES - LE GRAND RECUEIL tome III (1961 - nouvelle édition revue et corrigée par l'auteur en 1977): La grenouille - L'assiette.

Translations of Francis Ponge and original poems by Robert Bly © Robert Bly, 1990. All rights reserved.

My deepest thanks go to Heléne Frederickson, for her cogent and generous comments on these translations, and her patience during the many drafts. R.B.

PUBLISHED BY:
Owl's Head Press
428 Yale Avenue
Riverview, New Brunswick
CANADA E1B 2B5

DESIGN AND TYPESETTING:
Hawk Communication Associates Incorporated
Sackville, New Brunswick, Canada E0A 3C0

PRINTING:
The Tribune Press
Sackville, New Brunswick, Canada E0A 3C0

ISBN 0-920635-04-0

First Edition

COVER: Albrecht Dürer, "The Great Piece of Turf." Graphische Sammlung, Albertina, Vienna.

This book has been printed on acid-free, recycled paper.

CONTENTS
Part One

FRANCIS PONGE

Les arbres se défont à l'intérieur d'une sphère de brouillard 12
Trees Lose Parts of Themselves Inside a Circle of Fog 13
Les mûres 14
Blackberries 15
La fin de l'automne 16
The End of Fall 17
La grenouille 20
The Frog 21
L'huître 22
The Oyster 23
La bougie 24
The Candle 25
L'assiette 26
The Assiette (The Plate) 27
Les plaisirs de la porte 28
The Delights of the Door 29
Les trois boutiques 30
The Three Shops 31
Pluie 34
Rain 35

CONTENTS
Part 2

ROBERT BLY

A Chunk of Amethyst 40
An Oyster 41
A Potato 42
A Rock Crab 43
The Fog Horns at Port Townsend 44
An Ant Hill 46
The Cicada Husk 48
The Flounder 49
Peeling an Orange 51
The Mushroom 52

MY SURPRISE

I began to translate Francis Ponge's poems about twenty years ago, and each poem has been a delight. My greatest surprise came when I finally realized that Ponge does not believe in the unconscious. In other words he is not a Romantic.

The Romantic view of composition, which derives from the English and the German Romantics, means that the poet asks the unconscious, or the hidden man, or the hidden woman, or the latent intelligence, to enter the poem and contribute a few images that we may not fully understand. When I write a "seeing poem", I aim for some mysterious quality in the animal or object not entirely contained in human language.

Ponge does something completely different and absolutely astonishing to me. To him, the hidden qualities of a thing inhere in the history of language, where one finds the different meanings a word has carried over centuries. The study of words takes the place we reserve for the unconscious. In "Blackberries", we can read an amazing fusion of nature and human language.

Robert Bly

for James Hillman
investigator and inhaler of words

FRANCIS PONGE

LES ARBRES SE DÉFONT A L'INTÉRIEUR D'UNE SPHÈRE DE BROUILLARD

Dans le brouillard qui entoure les arbres, les feuilles leur sont dérobées; qui déjà, décontenancées par une lente oxydation, et mortifiées par le retrait de la sève au profit des fleurs et fruits, depuis les grosses chaleurs d'août tenaient moins à eux.

Dans l'écorce des rigoles verticales se creusent par où l'humidité jusqu'au sol est conduite à se désintéresser des parties vives du tronc.

Les fleurs sont dispersées, les fruits sont déposés. Depuis le plus jeune âge, la résignation de leurs qualités vives et de parties de leur corps est devenue pour les arbres un exercice familier.

TREES LOSE PARTS OF THEMSELVES INSIDE A CIRCLE OF FOG

Inside the fog that encloses the trees, they undergo a stripping.... Thrown into confusion by a slow oxidation, and humiliated by the sap's withdrawal for the sake of the flowers and fruits, the leaves, following the hot spells of August, cling less anyway.

The up and down tunnels inside the bark deepen, and guide the moisture down to earth so as to break off with the more animated parts of the tree.

The flowers are scattered, the fruits brought down. This giving up of their more animated parts, and even of parts of their body, has become, since their earliest days, a familiar pattern for trees.

LES MÛRES

    Aux buissons typographiques constitués par le poème sur une route qui ne mène hors des choses ni à l'esprit, certains fruits sont formés d'une agglomération de sphères qu'une goutte d'encre remplit.

*

    Noirs, roses et kakis ensemble sur la grappe, ils offrent plutôt le spectacle d'une famille rogue à ses âges divers, qu'une tentation très vive à la cueillette.
    Vue la disproportion des pépins à la pulpe les oiseaux les apprécient peu, si peu de chose au fond leur reste quand du bec à l'anus ils en sont traversés.

*

    Mais le poète au cours de sa promenade professionnelle, en prend de la graine à raison: «Ainsi donc, se dit-il, réussissent en grand nombre les efforts patients d'une fleur très fragile quoique par un rébarbatif enchevêtrement de ronces défendue. Sans beaucoup d'autres qualitiés, — *mûres*, parfaitement elles sont mûres — comme aussi ce poème est fait.»

BLACKBERRIES

On the typographical bushes that the poem forms along a road that leads neither out of the world of objects nor toward the spirit, certain fruits are composed of a gathering of spheres, filled with a drop of ink.

*

Blacks, pinks, and khakis all together, they present us with the spectacle of family members of distinct ages more than any strong desire to pick them.
I think the seeds are disproportionately big in comparison with the surrounding flesh; that's why the birds are not so interested. So little after all remains with them once the fruits have travelled through them from the beak to the anus.

*

But the poet on his professional walk learns something; he takes from the blackberries food for thought: "This is how," he says to himself, "the patient efforts of a flower — a delicate one — succeed, and generously, even though defended by a grim entanglement of brambles. Without many other virtues, they are ripe — yes, they are — they are finished blackberries, in the same way as this poem is now finished."

LA FIN DE L'AUTOMNE

Tout l'automne à la fin n'est plus qu'une tisane froide. Les feuilles mortes de toutes essences macèrent dans la pluie. Pas de fermentation, de création d'alcool: il faut attendre jusqu'au printemps l'effet d'une application de compresses sur une jambe de bois.

Le dépouillement se fait en désordre. Toutes les portes de la salle de scrutin s'ouvrent et se ferment, claquant violemment. Au panier, au panier! La Nature déchire ses manuscrits, démolit sa bibliothèque, gaule rageusement ses derniers fruits.

Puis elle se lève brusquement de sa table de travail. Sa stature aussitôt paraît immense. Décoiffée, elle a la tête dans la brume. Les bras ballants, elle aspire avec délices le vent glacé qui lui rafraîchit les idées. Les jours sont courts, la nuit tombe vite, le comique perd ses droits.

La terre dans les airs parmi les autres astres reprend son air sérieux. Sa partie éclairée est plus étroite, infiltrée de vallées d'ombre. Ses chaussures, comme celles d'un vagabond, s'imprègnent d'eau et font de la musique.

Dans cette grenouillerie, cette amphibiguïté salubre, tout reprend forces, saute de pierre en pierre et change de pré. Les ruisseaux se multiplient.

THE END OF FALL

What fall amounts to is really a cold infusion. The dead leaves of all herb species steep in the rain. But no fermenting goes on, no alcohol-making: one has to wait until spring to see the effect a compress has when applied to a wooden leg.

The counting of votes goes on chaotically. All the doors of the polling places fly open and slam shut. Into the wastebasket! Into the wastebasket! Nature rips up her manuscripts, tears down her library, knocks down the last fruits with long poles.

Then she rises crisply from her work table. Her height all at once seems unusual. Her hair undone, she has her head in the fog. Arms loose, she breathes in with ecstasy the icy wind that makes all her ideas clear. The days are short, the night falls swiftly, who needs comedy.

Earth floating among the other planets regains her serious look. Her sunlit side is narrower, invaded by clefts of shadow. Her shoes, like a hobo's, are great with water, and a source of music.

Inside this frogpond, or energetic amphibiguity, everything regains strength, hops from stone to stone, tries a new field. Streams increase.

Voilà ce qui s'appelle un beau nettoyage, et qui ne respecte pas les conventions! Habillé comme nu, trempé jusqu'aux os.

Et puis cela dure, ne sèche pas tout de suite. Trois mois de réflexion salutaire dans cet état; sans réaction vasculaire, sans peignoir ni gant de crin. Mais sa forte constitution y résiste.

Aussi, lorsque les petits bourgeons recommencent à pointer, savent-ils ce qu'ils font et de quoi il retourne, — et s'ils se montrent avec précaution, gourds et rougeauds, c'est en connaissance de cause.

Mais là commence une autre histoire, qui dépend peut-être mais n'a pas l'odeur de la règle noire qui va me servir à tirer mon trait sous celle-ci.

Here you see what is called a real soaking, a cleaning that cares nothing for respectability! Dressed as a naked man, soaked to the bone.

And it goes on, doesn't get dry right away. Three months of healthy reflecting goes on in this state; without any circulatory disaster, without bathrobe, without horsehair glove. But her strong constitution can take it.

And so, when the tiny buds begin to point, they know what they are doing and what is going on — and if they come out hesitatingly, numb and flushed, it is in full knowledge of why.

Ah well, but there hangs another tale — that may follow from, but certainly doesn't have the smell of, the black wooden ruler which I will use now to draw my line under this present story.

LA GRENOUILLE

Lorsque la pluie en courtes aiguillettes rebondit aux prés saturés, une naine amphibie, une Ophélie manchote, grosse à peine comme le poing, jaillit parfois sous les pas du poète et se jette au prochain étang.

Laissons fuir la nerveuse. Elle a de jolies jambes. Tout son corps est ganté de peau imperméable. A peine viande ses muscles longs sont d'une élégance ni chair ni poisson. Mais pour quitter les doigts la vertu du fluide s'allie chez elle aux efforts du vivant. Goitreuse, elle halète... Et ce cœur qui bat gros, ces paupières ridées, cette bouche hagarde m'apitoyent à la lâcher.

THE FROG

When rain like metal tips bounces off the sodden pastures, an amphibious dwarf, an Ophelia with empty sleeves, barely as large as a fist, rises at times from around the poet's feet, and then hurtles herself into the nearest pool.

Let this nervous one flee. How beautiful her legs are. A glove impermeable to water envelops her body. Barely flesh at all, her long muscles in their elegance are neither animal nor fish. In order to escape from my fingers the virtue of fluid allies in her with the battle of the life force. She puffs, widely goitered.... And this heart that beats so strongly, the wrinkly eyelids, the old woman's mouth, move me to set her free.

L'HUÎTRE

L'huître, de la grosseur d'un galet moyen, est d'une apparence plus rugueuse, d'une couleur moins unie, brillamment blanchâtre. C'est un monde opiniâtrement clos. Pourtant on peut l'ouvrir: il faut alors la tenir au creux d'un torchon, se servir d'un couteau ébréché et peu franc, s'y reprendre à plusieurs fois. Les doigts curieux s'y coupent, s'y cassent les ongles: c'est un travail grossier. Les coups qu'on lui porte marquent son enveloppe de ronds blancs, d'une sorte de halos.

A l'intérieur l'on trouve tout un monde, à boire et à manger: sous un *firmament* (à proprement parler) de nacre, les cieux d'en-dessus s'affaissent sur les cieux d'en-dessous, pour ne plus former qu'une mare, un sachet visqueux et verdâtre, qui flue et reflue à l'odeur et à la vue, frangé d'une dentelle noirâtre sur les bords.

Parfois très rare une formule perle à leur gosier de nacre, d'où l'on trouve aussitôt à s'orner.

THE OYSTER

The oyster, about as large as a medium-sized stone, has a rougher look, and a less consistent color, whitish in a dazzling way. It is a world bull-headedly sealed. You can open it, however; you must hold it then in the deep fold of a napkin, use a knife notched and not too honest, and try more than once. Fingers that are curious cut themselves, break their nails: it's not an elegant task. The knocks you give it leave whitish rings on the shell, halos of some kind.

Once inside, you will find an entire world, for drinking and for eating: beneath a *firmament* (to speak properly) of mother-of-pearl, the upper heavens slowly approach the lower heavens, making what is really only a pool, a viscous and greenish pillow that rises and falls as you smell and look, decorated at the edges with a fringe of blackish lace. Occasionally — it is rare — a beautiful expression rises in their mother-of-pearl throats, and you find good reason then to adorn yourself.

LA BOUGIE

La nuit parfois ravive une plante singulière dont la lueur décompose les chambres meublées en massifs d'ombre.

Sa feuille d'or tient impassible au creux d'une colonnette d'albâtre par un pédoncule très noir.

Les papillons miteux l'assaillent de préférence à la lune trop haute, qui vaporise les bois. Mais brûlés aussitôt ou vannés dans la bagarre, tous frémissent aux bords d'une frénésie voisine de la stupeur.

Cependant la bougie, par le vacillement des clartés sur le livre au brusque dégagement des fumées originales encourage le lecteur, — puis s'incline sur son assiette et se noie dans son aliment.

THE CANDLE

Night at times revives a curious plant whose light makes powerfully furnished rooms fall apart into clumps of shadow.

Its gold leaf stands unmoved attached to the hollow of a small column of alabaster by a pure black leafstalk.

The seedy moths attack it rather than attacking the too-high moon, that turns the woods to mist. But scorched in an instant or overstrained in the skirmish they all tremble on the brink of a mania close to stupor.

The candle, meanwhile, by the way its rays flicker on the book as it suddenly discharges its original gases urges the reader on — then bends over onto its plate and drowns in what has always fed it.

L'ASSIETTE

Pour le consacrer ici, gardons-nous de nacrer trop cet objet de tous les jours. Nulle ellipse prosodique, si brillante qu'elle soit, pour assez platement dire l'humble interposition de porcelaine entre l'esprit pur et l'appétit.

Non sans quelque humour, hélas (la bête s'y tenant mieux!), le nom de sa belle matière d'un coquillage fut pris. Nous, d'espèce vagabonde, n'y devons pas nous asseoir. On la nomma porcelaine, du latin — par analogie — *porcelana*, vulve de truie... Est-ce assez pour l'appétit?

Mais toute beauté qui, d'urgence, naît de l'instabilité des flots, prend assiette sur une conque... N'est-ce trop pour l'esprit pur?

L'assiette, quoi qu'il en soit, naquit ainsi de la mer: d'ailleurs multipliée aussitôt par ce jongleur bénévole remplaçant parfois en coulisse le morne vieillard qui nous lance à peine un soleil par jour.

C'est pourquoi tu la vois ici sous plusieurs espèces vibrant encore, comme ricochets s'immobilisant sur la nappe sacrée du linge.

Voilà tout ce qu'on peut dire d'un objet qui prête à vivre plus qu'il n'offre à réfléchir.

THE ASSIETTE (THE PLATE)

During our consecration here let's be careful not to make this thing that we use every day too pearly. No poetic leap, no matter how brilliant, can speak in a sufficiently flat way about the lowly interval that porcelain occupies between pure spirit and appetite.

Not without some humor, alas, (it fits its animal better), the name for its lovely matter was taken from a mollusc shell. And we, a gypsy species, are not to take a seat there. Its substance has been named porcelain, from the Latin — by analogy — *porcelana*, sow-vulva.... Is that good enough for your appetite?

But all beauty, which suddenly rises from the restlessness of the waves, has its true place on a seashell.... Is that too much for pure spirit?

And the assiette, whatever you say, rose in a similar way from the sea, and what's more was multiplied instantly by that free-spirited juggler in the wings who takes the place sometimes of the melancholic old man who tosses us with poor grace one sun per day.

That is why you see the assiette here in its numerous incarnations still vibrating as a skipped stone settles at last on the sacred surface of the tablecloth.

Here you have all that one can say about an object which contributes more for living than it offers for reflection.

LES PLAISIRS DE LA PORTE

Les rois ne touchent pas aux portes.

Ils ne connaissent pas ce bonheur: pousser devant soi avec douceur ou rudesse l'un de ces grands panneaux familiers, se retourner vers lui pour le remettre en place, — tenir dans ses bras une porte.

... Le bonheur d'empoigner au ventre par son nœud de porcelaine l'un de ces hauts obstacles d'une pièce; ce corps à corps rapide par lequel un instant la marche retenue, l'œil s'ouvre et le corps tout entier s'accommode à son nouvel appartement.

D'une main amicale il la retient encore, avant de la repousser décidément et s'enclore, — ce dont le déclic du ressort puissant mais bien huilé agréablement l'assure.

THE DELIGHTS OF THE DOOR

Kings don't touch doors.

They don't know this joy: to push affectionately or fiercely before us one of those huge panels we know so well, then to turn back in order to replace it — holding a door in our arms.

The pleasure of grabbing one of those tall barriers to a room abdominally, by its porcelain knot; of this swift fighting, body-to-body, when, the forward motion for an instant halted, the eye opens and the whole body adjusts to its new surroundings.

But the body still keeps one friendly hand on the door, holding it open, then decisively pushes the door away, closing itself in — which the click of the powerful but well-oiled spring pleasantly confirms.

LES TROIS BOUTIQUES

Près de la place Maubert, à l'endroit où chaque matin de bonne heure j'attends l'autobus, trois boutiques voisinent: Bijouterie, Bois et Charbons, Boucherie. Les contemplant tour à tour, j'observe les comportements différents à mes yeux du métal, de la pierre précieuse, du charbon, de la bûche, du morceau de viande.

Ne nous arrêtons pas trop aux métaux, qui sont seulement la suite d'une action violente ou divisante de l'homme sur des boues ou certains agglomérés qui par eux-mêmes n'eurent jamais de pareilles intentions; ni aux pierres précieuses, dont la rareté justement doit faire qu'on ne leur accorde que peu de mots très choisis dans un discours sur la nature équitablement composé.

Quant à la viande, un tremblement à sa vue, une espèce d'horreur ou de sympathie m'oblige à la plus grande discrétion. Fraîchement coupée, d'ailleurs, un voile de vapeur ou de fumée *sui generis* la dérobe aux yeux même qui voudraient faire preuve à proprement parler de cynisme: j'aurai dit tout ce que je peux dire lorsque j'aurai attiré l'attention, une minute, sur son aspect *pantelant*.

THE THREE SHOPS

Near the Place Maubert, at the spot where each morning early I wait for the bus, three shops stand side by side: Jewels, Coal and Firewood, Butcher. Observing them in turn, I notice how differently, it seems to me, metal, precious stones, coal, woodchunks, slices of raw meat behave.

We won't linger too long over the metals, which are only the result of man's exploitative or divisive influence on muds or on certain conglomerate rocks which by themselves had no such intentions, nor the precious stones, whose rarity correctly suggests that one give to them only a few exquisite words during a discourse on nature so equitably arranged.

As for the raw meat, a certain shiver as I look, a kind of horror or empathy obliges me to the greatest discretion. Moreover when freshly sliced a veil of steam or smoke *sui generis* screens them from the very eyes which would want to reveal certain, one might properly say, cynical thoughts. I will have said all that I can say when I have drawn attention for one minute to something *panting* in their appearance.

Mais la contemplation du bois et du charbon est une source de joies aussi faciles que sobres et sûres, que je serais content de faire partager. Sans doute y faudrait-il plusieurs pages, quand je ne dispose ici que de la moitié d'une. C'est pourquoi je me borne à vous proposer ce sujet de méditations: «1°) LE TEMPS OCCUPÉ EN VECTEURS SE VENGE TOURJOURS, PAR LA MORT. —2° BRUN, PARCE QUE LE BRUN EST ENTRE LE VERT ET LE NOIR SUR LE CHEMIN DE LA CARBONISATION, LE DESTIN DU BOIS COMPORTE ENCORE — QUOIQU'AU MINIMUM — UNE GESTE, C'EST-A-DIRE L'ERREUR, LE FAUX PAS, ET TOUS LES MALENTENDUS POSSIBLES.»

The contemplation of firewood and coal however is a source of delights as immediate as they are sober and certain, which I would be pleased to share. Without doubt that would require several pages, when in fact I have here only one half of one. That is why I set a limit and propose to you the following subject for your meditations: **1.** TIME THAT IS OCCUPIED WITH RADIUSES OF A CIRCLE ALWAYS REVENGES ITSELF, BY DEATH. **2.** BECAUSE IT IS BROWN, AND BROWN IS MIDWAY BETWEEN GREEN AND BLACK ON THE ROAD TO CARBON, THE WOOD'S DESTINY INVOLVES — THOUGH IN A SMALL DEGREE — A SERIES OF EXPLOITS, THAT IS TO SAY, ERROR ITSELF, MISTAKES, AND EVERY POSSIBLE MISUNDERSTANDING.

PLUIE

La pluie, dans la cour où je la regarde tomber, descend à des allures très diverses. Au centre c'est un fin rideau (ou réseau) discontinu, une chute implacable mais relativement lente de gouttes probablement assez légères, une précipitation sempiternelle sans vigueur, une fraction intense du météore pur. A peu de distance des murs de droite et de gauche tombent avec plus de bruit des gouttes plus lourdes, individuées. Ici elles semblent de la grosseur d'un grain de blé, là d'un pois, ailleurs presque d'une bille. Sur des tringles, sur les accoudoirs de la frenêtre la pluie court horizontalement tandis que sur la face inférieure des mêmes obstacles elle se suspend en berlingots convexes. Selon la surface entière d'un petit toit de zinc que le regard surplombe elle ruisselle en nappe très mince, moirée à cause de courants très variés par les imperceptibles ondulations et bosses de la couverture. De la gouttière attenante où elle coule avec la contention d'un ruisseau creux sans grande pente, elle choit tout à coup en un filet parfaitement vertical, assez grossièrement tressé, jusqu'au sol où elle se brise et rejaillit en aiguillettes brillantes.

RAIN

The rain falling into the courtyard where I watch adopts three manners, each distinct. Toward the center it is a delicate netting (or net) often with holes, a determined fall, though somewhat lethargic, the drops light enough, an eternal drizzle with no animal vigor, an obsessed particle of the pure meteor. Near the courtyard walls to right and left heavier drops are falling, energetically, less absorbed in the mass. A few seem big as a grain of wheat, others big as a pea, still others big as marbles. Flowing on the cornices and the stone sills, the rain moves horizontally, though underneath these same blocky barriers raindrops hang upside down shaped like bellied lozenges. Along the plain made by a tiny zinc roof which my position overhangs the rain makes a frail counterpane, given a silky texture by complicated streams that flow over the faintly visible undulations and humps of the roofing. The flow moves through a raingutter nearby with the difficulty of an insubstantial creek with no slope, then all at once it drops off in a ropelike thread utterly vertical, it has a thick enough weave, drops down to the pavement blocks, where it flies apart; and the fragments leap up, and are the tips of luminous laces.

Chacune de ses formes a une allure particulière; il y répond un bruit particulier. Le tout vit avec intensité comme un mécanisme compliqué, aussi précis que hasardeux, comme une horlogerie dont le ressort est la pesanteur d'une masse donnée de vapeur en précipitation.

La sonnerie au sol des filets verticaux, le glouglou des gouttières, les minuscules coups de gong se multiplient et résonnent à la fois en un concert sans monotonie, non sans délicatesse.

Lorsque le ressort s'est détendu, certains rouages quelque temps continuent à fonctionner, de plus en plus ralentis, puis toute la machinerie s'arrête. Alors si le soleil reparaît tout s'efface bientôt, le brillant appareil s'évapore: il a plu.

Each of these presences has its own manner, and each has its own particular sound. The rain, taken all together, runs like some complicated invention, fiercely, unpredictable and precise, a clockworks of which the moving agent is the weight associated with a given mass of water vapor in the process of precipitation.

The bell sound as the water-threads hit the stones, the gluppy sounds of the rainspouts, the light blows on the gong become complicated and resonate all together in a concerto never boring, never without true feeling.

When the stored energy in the spring is gone, certain wheels keep on running for a while anyway, more and more lethargically, then the whole thing comes to a stop. If the sun should reappear, the entire edifice vanishes, the light-filled device goes into thin air: well it rained.

ROBERT BLY

A CHUNK OF AMETHYST

Held up to the windowlight the amethyst has elegant corridors, that give and take light. The discipline of its many planes suggests that there is no use in trying to live forever. Its exterior is jagged, but in the inner house all is in order. Its corridors become ledges, solidified thoughts that pass each other.

This chunk of amethyst is a cool thing, hard as a dragon's tongue. The sleeping times of the whole human race lie hidden there. When the fingers fold the chunk into the palm, the palm hears organ music, the low notes that make the sins of the whole congregation resonate, and catches the criminal five miles away with a tinge of doubt.

With all its planes, it turns four or five faces toward us at once, and four or five meanings enter the mind. The exhilaration we felt as children returns.... We feel the wind on the face as we go downhill, the sled's speed increasing....

AN OYSTER

The oyster looks impenetrable and thuggy, and is the size of a baby mountain-lion's paw. Its surface is flaky, breaking off, crazily staked with little abdominal errors. There are waves here, as on gypsy skirts — concealing what?

Hands, as they move to open it, feel grainy, about to violate a privacy. Small flakes of subtle calcium fall away; they are the grief and surprise that come away from lips closed so long. We have to call for a knife, which is the gift of those who lived before us, a strong knife, the end simpleminded but without Puritanism; it arranges its hard-ended molecules so as to recapture the past, gallop up the valley, return the dead to their former lives.

The oyster body wets the tip of the nose as one tries to gulp it up...the lips feel satisfied, as if they deserve what they have received.

And when we see the two empty shells, we feel it is right to praise the naked life. The shells are ready now to be thrown away into gardens, or thrown back into the ocean, as simple plates of desire.

A POTATO

The potato reminds one of an alert desert stone. And it belongs to a race that writes novels of inspired defeat. The potato does not move on its own, and yet there is some motion in its shape, as if a whirlwind paused, then turned into potato flesh when a ghost spit at it. The skin mottles in spots; potato cities are scattered here and there over the planet. In some places papery flakes lift off, light as fog that lifts from early morning lakes.

Despite all the eyes, little light gets through. Whoever goes inside will find a weighty, meaty thing, damp and cheerful at the same time, obsessive as a bear that keeps crossing the same river. When the jaw bites into the raw flesh, both tongue and teeth pause astonished, as a bicyclist leans forward when the wind falls. The teeth say, "I could never have imagined it." The tongue says: "I thought from the cover that there would be a lot of plot...."

A ROCK CRAB

A rock crab lies firmly on a mess of greenish-brown seaweed; ocean water still gleams on his shell. He is matter, tangibleness, substantiality, a heavy downpouring of primitive light. The careless mottling on the top suggests desert forts.

A hand turns him over, and we see the underside, fierce like the underside of a desert. The six claws folded over the stomach are jointed segments of what has to be done, hard bits of necessity. The will is strong, living without mother or father, bony, unsentimental, even on the upper legs that slope like arms. Inside the girlish arms there is cold and muscular flesh, still visionary, washed at night when seawater carries its moony splashings through the claw tunnel.

If we get down on our knees and inhale the odor, we feel suddenly vulnerable, as when a scene from last night's dream returns; and we fall into the chill that floats around truth, the night salt.

THE FOG HORNS AT PORT TOWNSEND

The fog horn lasts about five seconds, and then there is a pause. We listen in silence, such waiting silence, the silence when the guests are about to arrive. The fog horn comes again. It says that the world will be born once more, surely it will. And its sound is the color of a brown dog, that lies for a long time before the fire.

The silence goes on a while...then a fainter horn farther off...another silence...then a third still farther away.... Then waiting again. The big horn comes. It says that a child has gotten lost on the mountain. Its sound has deep ocean loneliness in it, the long waves far at sea that no hulls pass over, and the moment at dawn when a whole city of sunlight rises up out of the ocean, and the moment at dusk when the saddened village, silent and surly, sinks with its golden roofs down.

There is a child lost on the mountain. It started down the wrong slope of the mountain, and that led it farther away from the others, even though they too were descending. Now the parents have not slept for days.

How do they know that the searchers will not go home this morning and drive the jeeps back down the logging roads? "It's no use; we covered the whole area." And if the child is found after having been away so long, who will keep it from going out again? And whose plate will it take?

AN ANT HILL

Ants working have heaped up these earth particles overnight, and each particle is a stomach traveller that has travelled all the way through Egypt. The travellers now lie all crowded together in their humility.

In the center of the hill a hole goes straight down, where humans cannot follow, down into the earth. It is the hole in the tip of the penis. Also it is the circular trapdoor in the kitchen floor that opens to the cellar. And the Japanese story says that if a woman drops a pancake, and then climbs down through the hole to retrieve it, she will meet the green and yellow giants, and will have to cook for them for five years.

This hole then must be death, though we agree that the ants did not fabricate death. They made the hole in order to see the light. As I watch on my knees, three ants rise, one after the other, and scramble up the crater sides. They move with jerky, electrical motions, fierce, intent on their task.

Last night in my dream several flying saucers appeared in the western sky to my mother and me.... And later, when they landed near where we stood, I opened a small vein or artery in my finger, so as to mingle my blood with the pale green blood of a plant.

When a son is born, the mother is always there. Death then must be something that we and our mother will experience together. She gave us a magic apple; it falls, and we get down on our knees to look for it. Glancing around, I can no longer see the three ants. They will go over the wide earth and return to this black hole, as to a friend's house.

THE CICADA HUSK

The cicada's husk remains attached to the underside of a log, the bottom log of a summer cabin. It hangs by its feet-husks. The head-husk, from which the head has already pulled away, amounts to a curious box, with bent turrets and double forehead, the consistency of rice paper; it is frail as those shrimp sheets that curl as they fall into boiling oil.

From the underside of the shoulder-husk, the first pair of absent legs sets out. The upper two sections of each leg are about an inch long, dry as a wheat stalk, thinned out by delicate terror. And there are more.

But the abdomen-husk — how much one feels the absentness of the abdomen, the guts, the stomach. Its husk is made of seven paper lanterns, or overlapping siding on an air house. The abdomen husk reminds one of those white Japanese paper lanterns that rich parents who want the children to leave hang in the garden for open house, so that the graduating seniors will feel the grandeur of the world.

THE FLOUNDER

The coarse grainy skin of the flounder makes one think of remarks made too coarsely, and too quickly. The color is the grayish pale brown of wolf paws. Its petulant, rubbery mouth widens gradually, and the flesh actually is an extension or widening of the mouth. The shape becomes a thick triangle; part way up, the fins continue in thought, in architectural fantasy, what the flesh itself decided not to do. Then at the upper peak, the fins begin to slope off, and by diminishing, make a second triangle sliding away toward the tail; and the tail too has its fin, a sort of afterthought.

It took some violence to get those eyes twisted around to one side – probably the sort of violence each family knows about. Whatever it was, the flounder ended floating along the ocean bottom, white side down, hoping not to be seen from above. The underside does not see the sun; it takes on the paleness of the cutworm, of the upper arms of women who always wear sleeved dresses.

It must be then that half of me stands here on shore, with my long line and casting rod, and the other half is down there, so that what stands above remains attached to what floats down there.

If Joseph had turned into a fish, and Egypt were a great river, then wouldn't Joseph, after he had fled from the Plantation Manager's wife, slipping away, naked, heading for the water, have glided about the legs of the thin cattle soon to rise from the river? He would swim slowly, as those fish whose long black feelers touch the muddy boulders. And if he became a man again, and slipped back into bed, would he be the brother on shore or the brother under the water?

PEELING AN ORANGE

The orange's hide is soft and grainy; and it has two navels, as if it were born once into this world, and once into the next. When the mouth opens to bite it, the teeth lose their hold and slide, and we feel abashed, as if a horse had gotten loose.

The teeth turn the orange over to the ten clever ones. The thumbnail enters first, and the nine friends hover around, offering to help. The orange skin now reveals its frightened white underside, as when citizens on the border lift their faces as the tanks approach. The right hand lifts a large flake to the lips; the teeth take it and the lips feel a sting for long afterward. So whoever dominates another has to put up with slightly numb lips. Fingers continue the job on their own, and soon the inner orange lies in the palm, looking scarred and naked.

What to do? The thumbs meet while the other eight hold it tight, and after a joint effort the orange falls apart, and the fingertips feel the wet of victory. The hand that holds the half orange inherits the mouth's instinctive longing; and modesty suggests the best solution, to swallow the naked thing. Soon the half-orange disappears, and the hand hovers, naked itself, wet, caught in the act, not sure what to do.... Perhaps pray or reach down toward the kitchen table for the other half.

THE MUSHROOM

This white mushroom comes up through the duffy lith on a granite cliff, in a crack that ice has widened. The most delicate light tan, it has the texture of a rubber ball left in the sun too long. To the fingers it feels a little like the tough heel of a foot.

One split has gone deep into it, dividing it into two half-spheres, and through the cut one can peek inside, where the flesh is white and gently naive.

The mushroom has a traveller's face. We know there are men and women in Old People's Homes whose souls prepare now for a trip, which will also be a marriage. There must be travellers all around us supporting us whom we do not recognize. This granite cliff also travels. Do we know more about our wife's journey or our dearest friends' than the journey of this rock? Can we be sure which traveller will arrive first, or when the wedding will be? Everything is passing away except the day of this wedding.